Contents

Series Title 3
Discipline: Accounting 3
Introduction 4
Balance Sheet Terms 5
T-Form Balance Sheet versus Vertical Balance Sheet 7
Working Capital 8
Accumulated Depreciation 9
Balance Sheet Template 10
Worked Tasks 11
   Task #1 11
   Task #2 11
   Task #3 11
Solutions ~ Worked Tasks 12
   Solution ~ Worked Task #1 12
   Solution ~ Worked Task #2 13
   Solution ~ Worked Task #3 14
Introductory Tasks 15
   Task #1 ~ Sid Vicious 15
   Task #2 ~ Jagged Edge 16
   Task #3 ~ Marie's Party Shop 17
Solutions ~ Introductory Tasks 18
   Task #1 ~ Sid Vicious 18
   Task #2 ~ Jagged Edge 18
   Task #3 ~ Marie's Party Shop 20
Fixed Assets 21
Revaluation of Fixed Assets 22
   Cost Model 22
   Revaluation Model 22
   Revaluation Reserve 23
   Depreciation after Revaluation 23
   Decrease in Fixed Asset 23
   Fixed Asset Derecognised 23
   Reversal of Revaluation 23

- Revaluation Increments/Decrements ... 24
- Impairment Test ... 25
- Goodwill ... 26
- Practical Tasks ... 27
  - Task #1 ~ The Wood Pile ... 27
  - Task #2 ~ Rippers Wrapping Service ... 28
  - Task #3 ~ Brad Loom Carpet Service ... 29
- Solutions ~ Practical Tasks ... 30
  - Task #1 ~ The Wood Pile ... 30
  - Task #2 ~ Rippers Wrapping Service ... 30
  - Task #3 ~ Brad Loom ... 33
- Author Background ... 35

Series Title

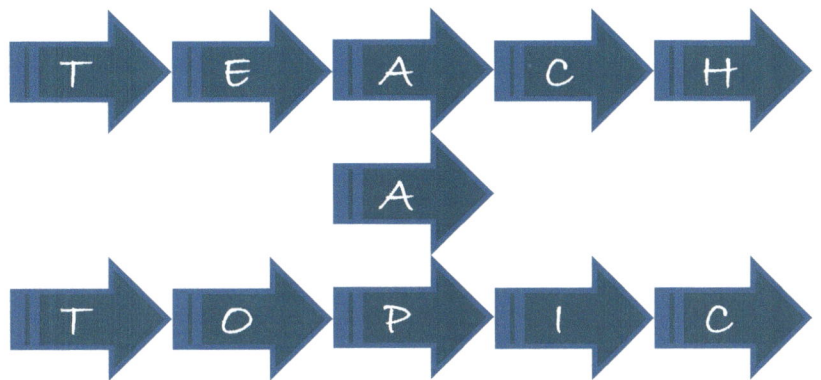

Discipline: Accounting

Topic: Balance Sheet

- Want to get straight to the topic?
- Want material 'lesson ready' or 'student ready'?
- Teach a Topic does just that.
- This book covers the Balance Sheet and follows this format:
  - What is a Balance Sheet – its purpose.
  - Understand the terms used in a Balance Sheet.
  - Template for a Balance Sheet – T format and vertical format (the most useful layout).
  - Worked tasks.
  - Solutions to worked tasks.
  - Explanation of what is a Fixed Asset.
  - Goodwill explained.
  - Revaluations explained and examples given.
  - Reserves shown in equity.
  - Practise tasks.
  - Solutions to practise tasks.

All that you need for a two or three hour lesson or for a thorough understanding on this topic.

Introduction

The Balance Sheet can also be called Statement of Financial Position (I will use both terms).

The Balance Sheet is a snapshot of a company's holdings at a given point in time. Because of this when writing one up you always state 'as at' and then the date. Usual dates for the end of a financial year might be:
- 31 March
- 30 June
- 31 December

The end of the financial year should be dictated by one of the following:
- the government department overseeing taxes eg Inland Revenue
- type of business activity eg end of a farming season
- academic year for learning institutions

It shows the assets owned by the company, the liabilities it owes to others and accumulated investments of the owner or owners. The Balance Sheet shows these figures on a specific date. In simple terms it shows where everything is.

The basic Balance Sheet formula is Assets = Liabilities + Equity. By definition the equation must balance. If the equation does not balance then an error has been made.

Assets are company resources. These include cash, inventory, accounts receivable, equipment, buildings, etc.

Liabilities are obligations the company must pay. These include accounts payable, bank debt, prepayment by customers, taxes and wages owed.

Equity is retained earnings, investment by owners and shares in the business.

Working Capital is another useful part of the balance sheet. Working capital is simply the assets and liabilities that a company works with on a daily basis. This statement gives an indication of a company's solvency or 'what shape are we in right now.' Basically it shows how 'liquid' the business is.

Liquidity is an important aspect of the Balance Sheet. Liquidity means being able to convert something to cash in a short period of time. Liquidity is important from a cash flow standpoint since it shows if a business can pay its bills.

Liquidity problems can bankrupt a business.

Liquidity is especially important when seeking a loan.

Balance Sheet Terms

Assets

Current Assets

cash
accounts receivable (also known as debtors)
inventories (also known as stock)
prepayments
accrued revenue

Current assets are assets that are either cash or can be converted into cash relatively quickly, usually within one accounting period. These are normally listed in order of liquidity – order of being able to be turned into cash. Examples:
- cash (bank)
- debtors (accounts receivable)
- stock (inventory)

Non-current Assets

Fixed Assets

These are assets are owned by the business, for the use in the business. They are of a long term nature and not intended for resale to customers. Their use is extended over a number of accounting periods. Examples:
- vehicles
- equipment
- plant (machinery)
- buildings
- land

Investments

Business funds invested for longer than one accounting period (shorter than that it would be shown under Current Assets). Examples of longer term investments would be:
- term deposit
- debentures
- shares in another business

Intangible Assets

These lack physical substance, ie they cannot be "seen", but they are still things of value which the business owns. They are a benefit gained by a business. They can include:
- goodwill – the value of a business over and above the total value of its tangible or physical assets perhaps from the amount of custom it has built up, or if a business was the only one of its kind in an area it would have a high goodwill and someone purchasing the business would expect high profits
- patents – the exclusive right to a certain product or process
- franchises – belonging to a network of businesses which generate high income because of marketing exposure

Liabilities

Current Liabilities

These are liabilities that are going to be repaid within one accounting period. Examples include:
- bank overdrafts
- accounts payable (also known as creditors) for the supply of goods and services received on credit
- revenue received in advance
- accrued expenses
- short-term loans to the business

Non-current Liabilities

Also known as long term liabilities. These are liabilities that are for longer than one accounting period. Examples are:
- long-term loans
- mortgages

Owner's Equity

Capital

We usually begin with an opening balance, add any additional capital brought in, subtract any losses or drawings, add profit to give a final capital figure. The format is as follows:

Opening Capital
plus Additional Capital
plus Profit
less Drawings
gives Closing Capital

Other term for owner's equity is proprietorship.

Notes:

A statement of Financial Position that has assets and liabilities classified under headings means:
- easier to read statement
- information is presented in a format that is useful for decision making
- separating current assets from other types of assets and current liabilities from other types of liabilities also enables us to have some idea of our cash flow or liquidity over the next accounting period.

- Current assets are classified in the order that they are most easily turned into cash ie their ease of liquidity. It is much easier to ask debtors to pay some money that they owe (perhaps!!!) than it might be to sell off extra stock.
- And – if you sell off extra stock it would usually be at a loss.
- In classifying the fixed assets, the smaller the book value of the item, the higher up the list it is placed eg a van at $7,000 would come before equipment at $54,000.
- Current Liabilities are listed in the order in which they should be repaid.

T-Form Balance Sheet versus Vertical Balance Sheet

> T-Form Statement of Financial Position (Balance Sheet) shows the equation –
> L + P = A

W Ash Cleaning Business
Statement of Financial Position
as at 31 March 2018

	$	$		$	$
Current Liabilities			**Current Assets**		
Bank overdraft	1,000		Cash	200	
Creditors (cleaning materials)	100	1,100	Stock (cleaning materials)	400	600
Long Term Liabilities			**Fixed Assets**		
Loan (L Ender)		500	Cleaning equipment	2,200	
			Van	2,500	4,700
Proprietorship					
Capital – W Ash		3,700			
		$5,300			$5,300

> Vertical Statement of Financial Position (Balance Sheet) shows the equation –
> P = A – L

> The vertical format is useful as it allows us to find the working capital.
> This is the acceptable layout these days.

W Ash Cleaning Business
Statement of Financial Position
as at 31 March 2018

	$	$	$
Proprietorship			
Capital – W Ash			3,700
This is represented by:			
Current Assets			
Cash	200		
Stock (cleaning materials)	400	600	
Less Current Liabilities			
Bank Overdraft	1,000		
Creditors (cleaning materials)	100	1,100	
Working Capital			(500)
Plus Fixed Assets			
Cleaning Equipment	2,200		
Van	2,500		4,700
			4,200
Less Term Liabilities			
Loan (L Ender)			500
			$3,700

Working Capital

One of the most important aspects of business management is making sure that there will be sufficient cash to meet ongoing expenses and current liabilities. The surplus of cash, once liabilities have been paid is called working capital. Working capital is calculated from this formula:

> **Working Capital = Current Assets – Current Liabilities**

Working capital is a common measure of a company's liquidity, efficiency, and overall health.

Positive working capital generally indicates that a company is able to pay off its short-term liabilities almost immediately. Negative working capital generally indicates a company is unable to do so. When there are decreases in working capital; it suggests a business is becoming overleveraged (that is borrowing or using other forms of credit), is struggling to maintain or grow sales, is paying bills too quickly, or is collecting accounts receivables too slowly. Increases in working capital, on the other hand, suggest the opposite.

One of the most significant uses of working capital is inventory. The longer inventory sits on the shelf or in the warehouse, the longer the company's working capital is tied up. The amount of working capital needs varies from industry to industry, especially considering how different industries depend on expensive equipment, use different accounting methods, and approach other industry-specific matters. For example, a company selling tractors to farmers would probably expect to have high levels of debtors over a number of months to work in with the farming seasons, while a supermarket should have little or no debtors but hold high levels of stock and a high level of creditors. For these reasons, comparison of working capital is generally most meaningful among companies within the same industry, and the definition of a "high" or "low" ratio should be made within this context.

To calculate a working capital ratio use this formula:

> **Current Assets / Current Liabilities**

A general rule is a ratio of 1:2. This means that for every dollar of current liability, the business has two dollars of current assets to make payments against those liabilities.

Examples:

current assets	4,700		current assets	3,500	
current liabilities	2,300		current liabilities	2,300	
working capital ratio	2.043		working capital ratio	1.522	
	1:2			1:050	
$2 available for every dollar of liability.		☑	50 cents available for every dollar of liability.		☒
current assets	11,200		current assets	8,250	
current liabilities	10,500		current liabilities	2,000	
working capital ratio	1.067		working capital ratio	4.125	
	1:1			1:4	
Just over a dollar available for every dollar of liability.		☒	$4 available for every dollar of liability.		
			Not good as do not need this much current assets.		☒

Accumulated Depreciation

When a business has fixed assets, they will depreciate each year. This depreciation will be 'written off' as an expense each year in the Income Statement.

However, in the Balance Sheet, each year's depreciation is added to the previous years' depreciation to become accumulated depreciation.

Accumulated depreciation is the gradual reducing of the value of the asset and this provides the business with the 'book value' of the asset.

After a number of years, the asset will be have no value 'on the books' for the asset; and therefore cannot be depreciated further. However, some businesses will still hold (keep) the asset because it has practical use and they will be able to claim running costs against that asset (just not depreciation).

Sometimes, an asset may be revalued upward – in which case the new value of the asset will be the base for a new depreciation expense and consequentially a new accumulated depreciation balance.

Examples of accumulated depreciation:

			Diminishing Value (DV)	
			Year 1	40,000 * 40%
				16,000
car	40,000			
less accumulated depreciation	16,000	24,000		
			Year 2	24,000 * 40%
				9,600
car	40,000			
less accumulated depreciation	25,600	14,400		
			Straight Line (SL)	
			Year 1	17,000 * 12%
				2,040
fixtures and fittings	17,000			
less accumulated depreciation	2,040	14,960		
			Year 2	17,000 * 12%
				2,040
fixtures and fittings	17,000			
less accumulated depreciation	4,080	12,920		

Straight line depreciation is always based on the historical cost (original cost) of the asset.

Diminishing value depreciation is based on the book value (the carrying value) of the asset. In the first year it will be on the historic cost as no other book value available.

Balance Sheet Template

Name of Company
Balance Sheet
as at 31 March 2018

	$	$	$
Owners Equity			
Capital 1 April 2017	120,000		
plus net profit	51,000	171,000	
less drawings		11,160	
Capital 31 March 2018			**$159,840**
This is represented by:			
Current Assets			
cash	10,000		
accounts receivable	15,000		
inventory	40,700		
prepayments	1,000		
accrued revenue	70	66,770	
less Current Liabilities			
bank overdraft	50		
accounts payable	20,500		
short-term loans	5,000		
accrued expenses	400		
revenue in advance	0	25,950	
Working Capital			40,820
plus Fixed Assets			
equipment	20,000		
less accumulated depreciation	2,000	18,000	
vehicle	27,000		
less accumulated depreciation	5,400	21,600	
building	58,000		
less accumulated depreciation	1,580	56,420	
plus Investments			
debenture in Company ABC		25,000	
plus Intangibles			
patent	70,000		
goodwill	55,000	125,000	246,020
less Non-current Liabilities			
long-term loan		40,000	
mortgage		87,000	127,000
			$159,840

Worked Tasks

Task #1

M Edicine, chemist, requires a fully classified Balance Sheet. The following are the assets and liabilities of the business at the end of the financial year.

Note: you will have to calculate the capital from: opening capital of $17,000 and profit for the year of 13,000. There were no drawings.

	$		$
stock	4,700	cash	100
bank overdraft	2,000	creditors	500
shop fittings	1,000	land and buildings	35,000
goodwill	1,700	mortgage	10,000

Task #2

S Heep, farmer, requires a fully classified Balance Sheet. He commenced the financial year with $77,500 in capital, he had drawings of $34,130 during the year and made $100,000 in profit after tax.

The following are the assets and liabilities of the business at the end of the financial year.

	$		$
tractor	3,000	farming equipment	5,000
shares in ACTO Freezing Co-op	2,570	bank	1,000
loan from Rural Bank	3,200	creditors	3,000
livestock	72,000	land and buildings	96,000
mortgage	30,000		

Task #3

Prepare a fully classified Balance Sheet of the following assets and liabilities of Hiskey's Self Service as at the end of this financial year. Been a rough year for trading – with the competition of supermarkets selling wines. Commenced the financial year with $70,000, made a profit after tax of $11,700 and had drawings of 7,300.

	$		$
land	18,000	buildings	25,000
fittings	10,000	creditors	6,000
mortgage	3,000	cash in till	200
Goldcorp debentures	3,000	office equipment	2,500
delivery van	12,000	goodwill	2,000
stock	12,000	bank overdraft	1,300

Solutions ~ Worked Tasks

Solution ~ Worked Task #1

M Edicine Chemist
Balance Sheet
as at 31 March 20xx

	$	$	$
Proprietorship			
Opening Capital		17,000	
plus Net Profit		13,000	
less Drawings			
Closing Capital			<u>30,000</u>
This is represented by:			
Current Assets			
cash	100		
stock	<u>4,700</u>	4,800	
less Current Liabilities			
creditors	500		
bank overdraft	<u>2,000</u>	<u>2,500</u>	
Working Capital			2,300
plus Fixed Assets			
shop fittings	1,000		
land and buildings	<u>35,000</u>	36,000	
plus Intangibles			
goodwill		<u>1,700</u>	<u>37,700</u>
			40,000
less Term Liabilities			
mortgage			<u>10,000</u>
			<u>$30,000</u>

Solution ~ Worked Task #2

S Heep
Balance Sheet
as at 31 March 20xx

	$	$	$
Proprietorship			
Opening Capital	77,500		
plus Net Profit	100,000	177,500	
less Drawings		34,130	
Closing Capital			**$143,370**
This is represented by:			
Current Assets			
bank	1,000		
livestock	72,000	73,000	
less Current Liabilities			
creditors	3,000		
bank loan	3,200	6,200	
Working Capital			66,800
plus Fixed Assets			
farming equipment	5,000		
tractor	3,000		
land and buildings	96,000	104,000	
plus Investments			
shares in ACTO Freezing Co-op		2,570	106,570
			173,370
less Term Liabilities			
mortgage			30,000
			$143,370

Solution ~ Worked Task #3

Hiskey's Self Service
Balance Sheet
as at 31 March 20xx

	$	$	$
Proprietorship			
Opening Capital	70,000		
plus Net Profit	11,700	81,700	
less Drawings		7,300	
Closing Capital			$74,400
This is represented by:			
Current Assets			
cash in till	200		
stock	12,000	12,200	
less Current Liabilities			
creditors	6,000		
bank overdraft	1,300	7,300	
Working Capital			4,900
plus Fixed Assets			
office equipment	2,500		
fittings	10,000		
delivery van	12,000		
buildings	25,000		
land	18,000	67,500	
plus Investments			
Goldcorp debentures		3,000	
plus Intangibles			
goodwill		2,000	72,500
			77,400
less Term Liabilities			
mortgage			3,000
			$74,400

Introductory Tasks

The following tasks are to demonstrate your understanding of the layout of the Balance Sheet.

Task #1 ~ Sid Vicious

Sid Vicious has his own band. He took over a band that had been performing for many years around the nightclubs and had a good reputation and following. He paid more than the assets of the business were worth - $25,000 in goodwill – but he thought it was well worth it.

It has been going for a year now and the band's is always in demand for performances. Sid is confident that he can now take over the accounts from his manager and present the reports himself. However, more difficult than he thought – so he asks you to write up the Balance Sheet for 30 June 2018.

At the end of the 2018 financial year the band has the following assets and liabilities:

bank	7,000
band equipment	50,700
creditors	7,150
van	22,470
capital (1 July 2017)	25,798
accum dep - van	12,000
accum dep - equip	11,800
outfits	4,290
hire purchase owing on drums	4,750

The above accumulated depreciation is already calculated for the current financial year.

A couple of venues that they played at in the New Year have still to pay up – they owe in total $15,200. He has invoiced them. Sid uses accrual accounting.

> Do you remember what accrual accounting is? You enter the figures into your accounts on invoice – not when you actually receive the income or make your payments. This allows a more realistic picture of earnings and revenue for particular periods.

He took out drawings for the year totalling $2,880; and a small overdraft with the bank of $1,000.

The band has been lucky this year with only one engagement failing to pay. They lost $500 over this.

Sid, ever the professional, has been taking tuition in learning the drums. He is learning heaps but it has cost him $1,000 this year.

The business made $58,042 (after tax) for the financial year. Sid didn't think this was too bad, considering each band member received a good wage (this would be shown in the Income Statement).

Because it is important to have forward bookings for the band, Sid is holding deposits from customers to the value of $17,000. This needs to be included in the Balance Sheet.

The band carries merchandising stock (tee-shirts and CDs) that they promote and sell at their shows. He has been in his garage and carried out a stock take and calculated the value at $10,000.

Task #2 ~ Jagged Edge

Jessica Sligh has trained as a hairdresser and worked in hair salons around her local town for many years. In April 2017 she felt it was the right time to set herself up in her own business. She purchased a business premise and called her hair salon 'Jagged Edge'.

She invested $40,289 of her own money as opening capital. During the year she did take out drawings of $28,000 which was probably not great since she only made $21,000 profit after tax for the year. Still, her clientele is increasing.

With the following details, prepare a Balance Sheet as at 31 March 2018. Use the vertical layout and include the working capital.

	$
driers	4,100
debtors	117
capital	40,289
mortgage	21,500
vehicle	23,740
cash float	200
creditors	400
fixtures and fittings	35,070
loan (due 1/1/2020)	2,800
bank	1,005
short-term loan	1,500
inventory	3,257

Depreciation for her fixed assets was:

Driers	$800
Fixtures and fittings	$4,400
Vehicle	$2,800

Use the formula OE = A - L to express the same information (you will need to total both current and non-current assets, and likewise current and non-current liabilities):

....
....
....

There are no intangible assets such as goodwill or patents. Can you give an explanation for this:

....
....
....
....
....

Task #3 ~ Marie's Party Shop

Marie owns a Party Shop that caters for birthdays, weddings and general celebratory events. Marie stocks a wide range of party items but she also organises occasions when customers require it. This means that she has a large amount of equipment that is used at party venues. Marie has been in her shop for two years.

On 1 April 2017, her capital investment was $34,060. Her net profit for the 2018 financial year is $15,000.

During the year, Marie decided to transfer her personal vehicle (valued at $11,000) into the business.

Marie has had difficulty with her cash flow this year: she has had to use an overdraft and take out a small loan.

In April 2017 Marie was thrilled to be granted a patent for her 'animal balloon maker' invention – this is worth $28,000 to her business. It had taken her two years to obtain this patent.

Below are her accounts for the 2018 financial year. Marie has already worked out her revenue and expenses; but she would like you to complete her Balance Sheet.

debtors	7,700	long term loan	16,000
fixtures and fittings	18,000	drawings	2,000
accumulated depreciation – f&f	1,800	creditors	24,100
van	17,250	inventory	17,710
accumulated depreciation – van	1,700	bank overdraft	1,000
cheque account	500	short-term loan	5,000
outdoor equipment	20,500	accum depn – outdoor equipment	2,000

Marie has a large amount of debt – particularly short-term. This is giving her negative working capital.

What are the implications (likely effect) on the business if this was to continue?

....
....
....
....

What can she do to help improve the situation?

....
....
....
....
....

Note:
Another name for debtors – accounts receivable.
Another name for creditors – accounts payable.

Solutions ~ Introductory Tasks

Task #1 ~ Sid Vicious

Sid Vicious
Balance Sheet
as at 30 June 2018

	$	$	$
Owner's Equity			
Opening Capital	25,798		
plus Net Profit	58,042	83,840	
less Drawings		2,880	
Closing Capital			$80,960
This is represented by:			
Current Assets			
bank	7,000		
debtors	15,200		
merchandising stock	10,000	32,200	
less Current Liabilities			
bank overdraft	1,000		
creditors	7,150		
hire purchase - drums	4,750		
revenue in advance	17,000	29,900	
Working Capital			2,300
plus Non-Current Assets			
Fixed Assets			
outfits		4,290	
band equipment	50,700		
less accumulated depreciation	11,800	38,900	
van	22,470		
less accumulated depreciation	12,000	10,470	
Intangibles			
goodwill		25,000	78,660
			$80,960

Note: Both the loss on band booking and the drums training Sid is having are shown in the Income Statement as expenses.

Task #2 ~ Jagged Edge

Jagged Edge Hairdresser
Balance Sheet
as at 31 March 2018

	$	$	$
Owner's Equity			
Capital	40,289		
plus Net Profit	21,000	61,289	
less drawings		28,000	
			$33,289
Represented by:			
Current Assets			
Cash Float	200		
Bank	1,005		
accounts receivable	117		
Inventory	3,257	4,579	
less Current Liabilities			
short-term loan	1,500		
accounts payable	400	1,900	
Working Capital			2,679
plus Non Current Assets			
driers	4,100		
less accumulated depreciation	800	3,300	
fixtures and fittings	35,070		
less accumulated depreciation	4,400	30,670	
vehicle	23,740		
less accumulated depreciation	2,800	20,940	54,910
			57,589
less Non-current Liabilities			
Loan (due 1/1/2013)		2,800	
Mortgage		21,500	24,300
			$33,289

Task #3 ~ Marie's Party Shop

Marie's Party Shop
Balance Sheet
as at 31 March 2018

	$	$	$
Proprietorship			
Capital 1 April 2017	34,060		
Additional capital	11,000		
plus net profit	15,000	60,060	
less drawings		2,000	
Capital 31 March 2018			**$58,060**
This is represented by:			
Current Assets			
cash	500		
accounts receivable	7,700		
inventory	17,710	25,910	
less Current Liabilities			
bank overdraft	1,000		
accounts payable	24,100		
short-term loans	5,000	30,100	
Working Capital			($4,190)
plus Non-Current Assets			
Fixed Assets			
outdoor equipment	20,500		
less accumulated depreciation	2,000	18,500	
van	17,250		
less accumulated depreciation	1,700	15,550	
fixtures and fittings	18,000		
less accumulated depreciation	1,800	16,200	50,250
Intangibles			
balloon patent			28,000
			74,060
less Term Liabilities			
long-term loan			16,000
			$58,060

Fixed Assets

Measurement (Cost and Valuation)

Tangible fixed assets are initially measured at cost (purchase price or production cost). Cost should include only those directly attributable costs that are incurred in bringing the asset to its present location and condition.

Examples of directly attributable costs include:
- acquisition costs (purchase costs)
- initial delivery and handling costs
- installation costs
- professional costs

Subsequent expenditure on fixed assets can only be capitalised if it enhances, restores or replaces the economic benefit of the asset.

While tangible fixed assets are shown on the balance sheet at market value, that is purchase price: at a later date these assets may become more valuable. If this occurs, fixed assets can be revalued. However if a policy of revaluation is adopted it must be consistently applied and must also be applied across a 'class' of assets. A 'class' means you need to revalue all of the vehicles the business owns, or all of the machinery. You cannot just pick and choose which vehicle or machinery to revalue.

I have gone into more detail on revaluation on the next page with some examples to assist.

Assets obtained by Hire Purchase/Finance Lease

If a company does not acquire a fixed asset outright but instead takes advantage of hire purchase or finance lease arrangements the correct method of accounting is to capitalise the asset at what would have been its cash cost, and to set up a liability to the finance house for the same sum.

The fixed asset is then accounted for as if it had been purchased outright.

Payments to the finance house are apportioned between interest and capital; the interest is charged to the profit and loss account and the capital payment is applied to reduce the liability. The interest apportionment must be calculated by the company, having regard to the outstanding amount of capital.

Note: This information is more for the next level of accounting – financial accounting. However, at an introductory level what you need to know is that it does not matter whether you 'paid cash' for the fixed asset or you are 'paying it off' on credit – it is still shown as if you own it on the Balance Sheet.

Disposal of Fixed Assets

When a fixed asset is disposed of, both the cost and accumulated depreciation to date are deducted from fixed assets brought forward and the net book value is written off. If the asset is sold the difference between the sale proceeds and the net book value is taken to Income Statement as either a gain or loss on disposal.

Revaluation of Fixed Assets

Revaluation of fixed assets is the process of increasing or decreasing their carrying value in case of major changes in fair market value of the fixed asset. International Financial Reporting Standards (IFRS) require fixed assets to be initially recorded at cost but they allow two models for subsequent accounting for fixed assets, namely the cost model and the revaluation model.

Cost Model

In the cost model the fixed assets are carried at their historical cost (original purchase cost) less accumulated depreciation and accumulated impairment losses. There is no upward adjustment to value due to changing circumstances.

For example: Machinery purchased for $200,000 (after VAT or GST taken off) and with a useful life of 20 years might use the straight line depreciation method. That would give $10,000 depreciation each year and the accumulated depreciation after three years would be $30,000 giving a book value of $170,000. This does not affect the historic cost ($200,000) of the machinery, only the book value ($170,000).

Revaluation Model

In the revaluation model an asset is initially recorded at cost but subsequently its carrying amount is increased to account for any appreciation in value. The difference between cost model and revaluation model is that revaluation model allows both downward and upward adjustment in value of an asset while cost model allows only downward adjustment due to impairment loss.

If we use the above example, after three years of use, the business carries out a revaluation on the machinery which gives a fair value of $190,000. The book value (carrying amount) of the machinery at that time is $170,000 (three years of depreciation at $10,000 per year). An upward adjustment needs to be made to the machinery account. It is recorded through a journal entry:

	Dr	Cr
Machinery	20,000	
Revaluation reserve		20,000

Under this approach, one must continue to revalue fixed assets at sufficiently regular intervals to ensure that the carrying amount (book value) does not differ materially from the fair value in any period. Under IFRS, once every three to five years is acceptable for revaluations, unless an asset is specialised or susceptible to changes in the market place such as technological assets; when possibly a revaluation every year might be necessary.

When a fixed asset is revalued, the simplest way to deal with the accumulated depreciation is to eliminate the accumulated depreciation against the gross carrying amount of the newly-revalued asset.

To work out the new value there are a number of options:
- Market-based appraisal by a qualified valuer.
- Discounted future cash flows (this method is more involved – you would study this at a financial accounting level).
- An estimated replacement cost of the asset.
- Use the technical expertise of an employee to assess its worth.

Revaluation Reserve

Upward revaluation is not considered a normal gain and is not recorded in the Income Statement; rather it is directly credited to an equity account called revaluation surplus or reserve. The **Revaluation Reserve** holds all the upward revaluations of a company's assets until those assets are disposed of.

Basically, if you are going to 'lift' the value of an asset, to balance that increase in fixed assets, another account is created in Owner's Equity – Asset Revaluation Reserve of ARR. The ARR is a 'paper' account.

However, if the increase reverses a revaluation decrease for the same asset that had been previously recognized in profit or loss, recognize the revaluation gain in profit or loss to the extent of the previous loss (thereby erasing the loss).

Depreciation after Revaluation

The depreciation in periods after revaluation is based on the revalued amount. In the above case of machinery, depreciation for year four shall be the new carrying amount divided by the remaining useful life or $190,000/17 which equals $11,176.

Decrease in Fixed Asset

If a revaluation results in a decrease in the carrying amount of a fixed asset, recognise the decrease in the Income Statement. However, if there is a credit balance in the revaluation surplus for that asset, you need to firstly 'take out' the amount of loss (remember it is a paper account) and then if there is still a loss, then the balance loss is recognised in the Income Statement.

Fixed Asset Derecognised

If a fixed asset is derecognized (that is the fixed asset is no longer on the books), transfer any associated revaluation surplus to retained earnings.

Reversal of Revaluation

If a revalued asset is subsequently valued down due to impairment, the loss is first written off against any balance available in the revaluation reserve and if the loss exceeds the revaluation surplus balance of the same asset the difference is charged to the Income Statement as an impairment loss.

Suppose, with our above example, the business two years' later, revalues the machinery again to find out that the fair value should be $160,000. The previous carrying amount was $190,000 minus 2 years depreciation of $22,352 which amounts to $167,648.

The carrying amount exceeds the fair value by $7,648 so the account balance should be reduced by that amount. We already have a balance of $20,000 in the revaluation surplus account related to the same piece of machinery, so no impairment loss will go to the Income Statement. The journal entry would be:

	Dr	Cr
Revaluation Reserve	7,648	
Machinery		7,648

Had the fair value been $140,000 the excess of carrying amount over fair value would have been $27,648. In that situation the following journal entry would have been required:

	Dr	Cr
Revaluation Reserve	20,000	
Impairment Loss	7,648	
Machinery		20,000
Accumulated Impairment Losses		7,648

The basis for revaluing assets is fair value. However, the writing down of the value of an impaired asset is not a revaluation.

Revaluation Increments/Decrements

Normally, net asset revaluation increments/decrements are credited/debited to the asset revaluation reserve for each asset class. However:

- where there are insufficient credits in the relevant asset revaluation reserve to absorb a revaluation decrement, the excess is recorded as an expense; and
- where a revaluation increment reverses a previous decrement that was expensed, the increment is recorded as revenue.

Note:

Asset revaluation reserves must never have a negative balance.

Impairment Test

Entities that are required to produce general purpose financial reports but which choose not to revalue non-current assets are required to conduct an annual impairment test of those assets. Assets are the future economic benefits controlled by the entity, so entities must assess whether anything has happened to jeopardise those benefits.

Impairment can be caused by a number of events:
- passage of time
- greater than expected use
- obsolescence or physical damage
- changes in technology
- changes in market tastes
- legal and economic forces
- damage

In addition, a review for impairment of fixed assets and goodwill should be carried out if events or changes in circumstances indicate that the carrying amount of the fixed asset or goodwill may not be recoverable.

Examples of events indicating impairment:
- Current period losses, or net cash outflows, combined with either past losses or net cash outflows, or an expectation of continuing losses or cash outflows
- A significant decline in market value
- Major loss of key employees

These events, if serious enough, could result in the carrying value of an asset being stated at **more** than its recoverable amount[1], thus misleading the reader of the financial statements.

Following an impairment review, the assets concerned should be stated at the lower of their brought forward carrying value and their recoverable amount. Recoverable amount is the *higher* of:

Net Realisable Value	and	**Value in use**
Amount at which assets could be disposed of less any direct selling costs.		The present value of future cash flows obtainable as a result of an asset's continued use, including those from its ultimate disposal.

If the test discloses that the recoverable amount is less than carrying value, the entity is required to write the asset down to recoverable amount. The amount of the write-down is known as an **impairment loss**, and is recognised as an expense in the Income Statement.

An impairment review of tangible fixed assets where no depreciation charge is made on the grounds of immateriality or where the estimated remaining useful life of the asset exceeds 50 years, should be undertaken every year.

---

[1] The greater of net market value and value-in-use ie the greater of its selling price (after selling costs are deducted) and the future expected earnings of the asset.

Goodwill

Goodwill is commonly defined as the value attached to the probability that customers will come back.

People develop habits of dealing with businesses that are convenient and have proved satisfactory in the past. Provided that circumstances do not change, these people become regular customers of these businesses.

A person wishing to commence business has to decide whether to purchase one already established or start a completely new enterprise.

Should he or she wish to adopt the first alternative he or she must reach an agreement with the vendor on the consideration or contract price and the vendor may seek a price that is more than the total valuation of the physical assets less liabilities acquired. This relates to goodwill.

Another way of putting this: the assets of the business are its 'fair value' and then the market price is what a person will buy the business for. The difference can be classified as the goodwill.

Market Value = Fair Price + Goodwill

This amount charged for goodwill could be the consequence of:
- taking over a business already set up and therefore setting up costs will not have to be incurred
- a business with a good reputation
- being part of a franchise group which offers a known and established name association and other benefits
- good site visibility for business
- established customers
- a good record of profits or other proven advantages eg good business practices
- manufacturing efficiency
- satisfactory relations between the employees and the management, which contribute to earnings through effective employee service and the reduction of loss through labour turnover
- adequate sources of capital and a credit standing which is reflected in low money costs
- monopolistic privileges

Nobody can determine an exact value for goodwill. An asset such as cash on hand, stock, investments or plant can be valued exactly, but goodwill is invariably valued as a consequence of bargaining between buyer and seller. It will depend how keen the purchaser is to buy the business, or how desperate the owner is to sell.

On the other hand it may be calculated on the basis of past or anticipated earnings (net profit before taxation) of the business. When a purchaser of the business pays a **price for goodwill s/he is not paying for the earnings of the past, but for probable earnings of the future**, however the earnings of the past may furnish the best available evidence of the earnings of the future.

Here is one example: some multiple of the average past annual net profits after adjustment for unusual and non-recurring items and anticipated changes affecting future revenue end expense.

> Assume that the average adjusted earnings for 5 years prior to the date of sale has been $10,000, and that goodwill is to be valued at twice the average earnings.
>
> Goodwill = $10000 x 2 = $20000

Practical Tasks

Task #1 ~ The Wood Pile

Lance Wood is a sole trader and owns a retail outlet called The Wood Pile, that specialises in wooden toys.

Lance employs his nephew – Wal Nutt on a part-time basis. Some of the shops' toys are imported but where he can Lance sources New Zealand sustainable timber products.

Lance has been in business for one year and he has asked you to prepare end of year financial statements for him. The ledger balances for his Balance Sheet at the end of the accounting period are:

bank	2,210
accumulated depreciation – fixtures and fittings (as at 1 April 2017)	7,000
mortgage	80,000
accounts receivable	500
bank overdraft	1,500
fixtures and fittings	18,200
van	25,500
accumulated depreciation – van (as at 1 April 2017)	10,200
PAYE owing to Inland Revenue	807
accounts payable	2,580
shop	170,000
capital	35,000
loan	18,000
petty cash	50
drawings	1,000
accumulated depreciation – shop (as at 1 April 2017)	7,500

Create a Balance Sheet for The Wood Pile as at 31 March 2018.

Net profit for the financial year is $47,363.

You will need to calculate depreciation and add it to the previous accumulated depreciation.
Depreciation: van is 40% DV (diminishing value)
Fixtures and fittings: 10% SL (straight line)
Shop: 3% SL (straight line)

Remember: DV depreciation is calculated on the book value not on the historic value as SL is.

A provision for doubtful debts of 5% is to be established – to be based on the closing figure of accounts receivable.

The closing stock figure is $5,100.

Prepayments are to be recorded for $1,225.

Lance has also taken in $770 in deposits for items that he has 'on order' from overseas; but hasn't yet been able to deliver.

Task #2 ~ Rippers Wrapping Service

Kelsey started up business in July 2017 with a stall in the city's main Mall to wrap gifts. She invested all of her savings of $5,050 and her vehicle valued at $20,750.

She is not too sure if the business will succeed; but she has kept track of all the accounts and worked out how much depreciation she can claim. Equipment to be calculated at 30% straight-line, the selling stall at 7% straight-line, the vehicle at 35% diminishing value.

Now it is time to discover whether the enterprise is viable. Kelsey really does like being outside and meeting people and of course, making peoples' purchases 'pretty'.

Profit after tax for the year is $33,712.

During the year, Kelsey had a small lottery win of $1,500 – and she put this money into your business as capital.

She paid herself a wage (see below); but also took out of the business $400 a month as drawings.

During the year, her business non interest bearing cheque account had a good balance, so she decided to transfer $15,000 of the funds into a term investment account under the business name.

She is in a bit of a muddle: she has all of the following accounts and but only wants the Balance Sheet detail. She is not sure what belongs in the Income Statement and what belongs in the Balance Sheet.

bank overdraft	500	equipment	4,250
cell phone charges	235	purchases	12,580
wage	12,000	returns in (sales returns)	4,750
vehicle	20,750	cleaning fee	1,000
bank loan (long term)	11,500	creditors	1,000
sales	43,900	Mall charge for the stall site	12,000
advertising	430	interest on loan	55
short-term loan	2,500	debtors	4,000
bank	1,700	insurance	750
donations	$50	stall	29,000
stock (closing)	2,580	lawyer fee	1,125
contribution to Mall Xmas fund	500		

Required:
- Extract the Balance Sheet items.

- Calculate the amount of depreciation for this first year of business. **Note:** this will be the same figure for the accumulated depreciation since it is the first year of business.

- Prepare the Balance Sheet for the current year. Use the vertical layout and include calculation for Working Capital.

Task #3 ~ Brad Loom Carpet Service

Brad Loom runs a carpet laying business that he purchased as a well established business a couple of years' ago. It is fairly successful based on the previous year's trading but he does have a high level of debt and a high level of working capital.

- Create a Balance Sheet for this financial year from the following information extracted from Brad's accounts:

	$
bank	2,000
accounts receivable	24,000
accounts payable	83,690
short-term loan	6,000
mortgage	100,000
petty cash	500
capital	170,000
shop fittings	47,400
vans	70,000
showroom	80,000
land	120,000
prepayments	240
accumulated depreciation – shop fittings	8,050
revenue in advance (customer deposits)	11,000
office equipment	10,000
shares in NZ Oil	5,000
bank overdraft	7,000
goodwill	40,000
carpet stock	203,000
term loan	50,500
accrued expenses	1,080
net profit	156,100
drawings	14,000
accumulated depreciation – office equipment	2,750
accumulated depreciation – showroom	5,870
accumulated depreciation – vans	14,280
accrued revenue (dividend from NZ Oil)	180

Note: 'Accrued revenue' and 'prepayments' are current assets. 'Accrued expenses' and 'revenue in advance' are current liabilities. (You learn about these accounts in Balance Day Adjustments/Trial Balance). Basically, they are 'temporary' accounts for monies the business is holding, is owing or is owed.

Analyse and comment on Brad's level of debt as it relates to his working capital and also long-term debt and prospects for solvency within the next couple of years:

....
....
....
....
....
....

Solutions ~ Practical Tasks

Task #1 ~ The Wood Pile

The Wood Pile
Balance Sheet
as at 31 March 2018

	$	$	$
Owners Equity			
capital	35,000		
plus net profit	47,363	82,363	
less drawings		1,000	
closing capital			**$81,363**
This is represented by:			
Current Assets			
petty cash		50	
bank		2,210	
accounts receivable	500		
less provision for doubtful debts	25	475	
stock		5,100	
prepayments		1,225	9,060
less Current Liabilities			
IRD - PAYE		807	
bank overdraft		1,500	
accounts payable		2,580	
income in advance		770	5,657
Working Capital			3,403
plus Non-current Assets			
fixtures and fittings	18,200		
less acc depreciation	8,820	9,380	
van	25,500		
less acc depreciation	16,320	9,180	
shop	170,000		
less acc depreciation	12,600	157,400	175,960
			179,363
less Non-current Liabilities			
loan		18,000	
mortgage		80,000	98,000
			$81,363

		Accum Depn 1-Apr-17	New Depreciation	Accum Depn 31-Mar-18
fixtures & fittings	10%	7,000	1,820	8,820
shop	3%	7,500	5,100	12,600
van	40%	10,200	6,120	16,320

van ← historic cost 25,500
accum depn 10,200 → book value 15,300
apply 40% to this figure

Task #2 ~ Rippers Wrapping Service

Rippers Wrapping Service
Balance Sheet
as at 30 June 2018

	$	$	$
Owner's Equity			
Capital	25,800		
plus net profit	33,712		
plus additional capital	1,500	61,012	
less drawings		4,800	**$56,212**
This is represented by:			
Current Assets			
Bank	1,700		
Debtors	4,000		
Stock	2,580	8,280	
less Current Liabilities			
bank overdraft	500		
creditors	1,000		
short-term loan	2,500	4,000	
Working Capital			4,280
plus			
Fixed Assets			
equipment	4,250		
less accumulated depreciation	1,275	2,975	
vehicle	20,750		
less accumulated depreciation	7,263	13,487	
stall	29,000		
less accumulated depreciation	2,030	26,970	
Investments			
Term investment		15,000	58,432
			62,712
less Non-Current Liabilities			
long-term bank loan			6,500
			$56,212

Additional Notes to this task:

- All other items in the accounts shown in the task belong in the Income Statement as either revenue (sales) or expenses.

- Depreciation was calculated as follows:

Depreciation

		SL	DV	
stall	29,000	7%		2,030
equipment	4,250	30%		1,275
vehicle	20,750		35%	7,263

Task #3 ~ Brad Loom

Brad Loom's Carpet Service

Balance Sheet
as at 31 March 2018

	$	$	$
Owner's Equity			
Opening Capital	170,000		
plus Net Profit	156,100	326100	
less Drawings		14,000	
Closing Capital			**$312,100**
This is represented by:			
Current Assets			
petty cash	500		
bank	2,000		
accounts receivable	24,000		
stock	203,000		
prepayments	240		
accrued revenue	180	229,920	
less Current Liabilities			
bank overdraft	7,000		
accounts payable	83,690		
short-term loan	6,000		
accrued expenses	1,080		
revenue in advance	11,000	108,770	
Working Capital			121,150
plus Non-Current Tangible Assets			
Fixed Assets			
office equipment	10,000		
less acc dep - office equipment	2,750	7,250	
shop fittings	47,400		
less acc dep - shop fittings	8,050	39,350	
vans	70,000		
less acc dep - vans	14,280	55,720	
showroom	80,000		
less acc dep - showroom	5,870	74,130	
land		120,000	
Investments			
shares in NZ Oil		5,000	
Intangibles			
goodwill		40,000	341,450
			462,600
less Non-current Liabilities			
term loan		50,500	
mortgage		100,000	150,500
			$312,100

Comments about Brad's level of debt, prospects for solvency.

Brad has to carry a large amount of stock – that is what his business is about. However, he has a high level of accounts payable (creditors) that need to be paid usually within one month. If he had a couple of months' of poor trading, those creditors would still need to be paid; but even before them his bank would be pushing for him to clear his bank overdraft or pay interest on his short-term bank loan.

What Brad needs to do is reduce down his accounts receivable sufficiently by calling in those customers to make payments, perhaps encourage more cash sales. Do not reduce stock prices though as he needs the mark up to continue in business. If he can clear some accounts receivable, those funds could help reduce his bank overdraft and short-term loan.

Long term, he needs to reduce his term loan and mortgage – each has to have regular payments made against them, and taking out short-term loans and overdrafts are not going to solve the issue.

Without viewing the Income Statement, the only other points you might make are:
- Is he paying himself a wage? If so, why is he taking out drawings?
- The profit seems reasonable, but why is there not more funds in the bank?
- Does he have a sufficient mark up on his stock? That is the difference between what he buys his carpet for and what he sells it for.

The working capital is high, but again that might be because of the high stock price (carpets). Because he has been in business a couple of years his working capital ratio should be around $2 of current assets to $1 of current liabilities. Brad's working capital ratio is all right at $2.11 current assets. How do we work that out?

Total current assets:	$229,920
Total current liabilities:	$108,770

Divide the current assets by the current liabilities:	229,920/108,770
Equals:	2.11
Change that to a ratio:	1:2.11

This means: for every $1 of current liabilities, there is $2.11 of current assets to pay for them.

Author Background

I am a trained teacher and have a Master's degree, diplomas in computing and belong to the Institute of Management. I have been a teacher/lecturer for the past 30 years: firstly nine years at secondary level then for the past 21 years at tertiary institutions teaching to graduate level. Over these many years I have purchased hundreds of technical texts. What I have found though is (apart from a couple of texts), I was probably only 'pulling out' one or two areas of information from each book and they have then just sat on my study shelves.

About five years ago, I finally decided there had to be a different way to approach each of my lessons. This is when I created topic booklets. Each booklet represents all that I need for a two hour teaching session: theory, worked tasks, practical tasks and solutions and a review of the lesson. Occasionally of course, dependent on the needs of the students, there might be a need to have another session on a topic – but again, I could use the same format but with additional practical tasks.

These topic booklets are my teaching plan/my guide – but of course it is equally important on how it is presented in front of the students. If the material is there and you are comfortable with it, then you are relaxed in front of the students. Dependent upon the discipline or topic, I still use PowerPoint and other interactive resources.

It is my intention to make life easier for teachers/tutors. If there is a topic that you would like covered; I would welcome suggestions and it would be my pleasure to create a topic book for you (so long as it was within my expertise of course).

Quite importantly, if you find errors in my work; or do not understand my rationale behind a concept – I would be most grateful if you drew that to my attention. Note: For introductory concept teaching in this discipline, I have omitted sales tax (VAT or GST); as I feel there is sufficient learning with new concepts before introducing the 'applied' aspects.

I have taken great care not to infringe on other people's work; although it is hard not to pick up ideas and to develop from those ideas. Likewise, there is so much generic material that I have found repeated in a number of different publications. The amount of help that in recent years is made available on the Internet is a credit to the generosity of the people who provide it (both written ideas, tutorials, YouTube) and again, I have gained knowledge from these sources. However, if anyone feels that my theory or task storylines are too similar to their own – then please let me know and I will alter my material accordingly. I have purchased my own graphics software (IMSI) but occasionally also use free graphics from Google. Any drawings or cartoon strips are my own.

What I have found is that a self-contained lesson topic is what is needed – and that is why and how I have developed my 'lesson plans'.

I hope that you find these topic books helpful.

Contact Details:

Judith Pope
teachatopic@gmail.com

© J Pope 2018

www.ingramcontent.com/pod-product-compliance
Lightning Source LLC
Chambersburg PA
CBHW051820210526
45473CB00005B/1674